Pet Care

Dalmatians

Kelley MacAulay & Bobbie Kalman
Photographs by Marc Crabtree

Crabtree Publishing Company
www.crabtreebooks.com

Dalmatians

A Bobbie Kalman Book

Dedicated by Michael Hodge
To Monty. You're a very good girl.

Editor-in-Chief
Bobbie Kalman

Writing team
Kelley MacAulay
Bobbie Kalman

Substantive editor
Kathryn Smithyman

Editors
Molly Aloian
Michael Hodge
Rebecca Sjonger

Design
Margaret Amy Salter

Production coordinator
Heather Fitzpatrick

Photo research
Crystal Foxton

Consultant
Dr. Michael A. Dutton, DVM, DABVP, Weare Animal Hospital,
www.weareanimalhospital.com

Special thanks to
Katherine Kantor, Alexander Makubuya, Lakme Mehta-Jones,
Owen Mehta-Jones, Shilpa Mehta-Jones, Samara Parent, Bailee Setikas,
Shelbi Setikas, Sheri Setikas, Katrina Sikkens, Michael and Jenn Hodge
and Monty, Danny Schafer and Reilly and Cruiser

Photographs
All photos by Marc Crabtree except:
© Christie's Images/Corbis: page 6
Photo Courtesy of HatTrick Dalmatians: page 29
Adobe Image Library: pages 14, 15 (bottom)
Comstock: page 21 (meat, milk, and egg)
Digital Stock: page 7
Ingram Photo Objects: page 21 (chocolate)

Illustrations
Margaret Amy Salter: page 21

Library and Archives Canada Cataloguing in Publication

MacAulay, Kelley
    Dalmatians / Kelley MacAulay & Bobbie Kalman.

(Pet care)
Includes index.
ISBN-13: 978-0-7787-1761-4 (bound)
ISBN-10: 0-7787-1761-5 (bound)
ISBN-13: 978-0-7787-1793-5 (pbk.)
ISBN-10: 0-7787-1793-3 (pbk.)
    1. Dalmatian dog--Juvenile literature. I. Kalman, Bobbie, date.
II. Title. III. Series: Pet care

SF429.D3M33 2006   j636.72   C2006-904092-3

Library of Congress Cataloging-in-Publication Data

MacAulay, Kelley.
    Dalmatians / Kelley MacAulay & Bobbie Kalman ; photographs by Marc
Crabtree.
        p. cm. -- (Pet care)
    Includes index.
    ISBN-13: 978-0-7787-1761-4 (rlb)
    ISBN-10: 0-7787-1761-5 (rlb)
    ISBN-13: 978-0-7787-1793-5 (pb)
    ISBN-10: 0-7787-1793-3 (pb)
    1. Dalmatian dog--Juvenile literature. I. Kalman, Bobbie. II. Title.
III. Series.
    SF429.D3M33 2006
    636.72--dc22
                                                    2006018063

Crabtree Publishing Company

www.crabtreebooks.com   1-800-387-7650

Published in Canada
Crabtree Publishing
616 Welland Ave.
St. Catharines, ON
L2M 5V6

Published in the United States
Crabtree Publishing
PMB16A
350 Fifth Ave., Suite 3308
New York, NY 10118

Published in the United Kingdom
Crabtree Publishing
White Cross Mills
High Town, Lancaster
LA1 4XS

Published in Australia
Crabtree Publishing
386 Mt. Alexander Rd.
Ascot Vale (Melbourne)
VIC 3032

Contents

What are dalmatians?

Dalmatians are a **breed**, or type, of dog. Dogs are **mammals**. Mammals are animals that have **backbones**. A backbone is a row of bones in the middle of an animal's back. Mammals also have hair or fur on their bodies. A baby mammal drinks milk from its mother's body.

A dalmatian's body

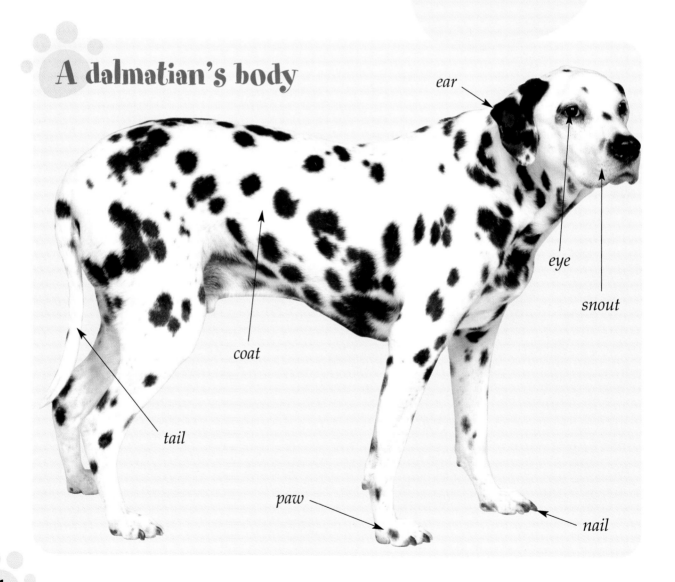

ear

eye

snout

coat

tail

paw

nail

Dandy dalmatians

Dalmatians are large dogs. Most dalmatians grow to be between 19 and 23 inches (48-58 cm) tall. They usually weigh between 40 and 65 pounds (18-29 kg). Dalmatians are known for their spotted coats. The coats are white with either black spots or dark-brown spots.

Dalmatians usually live for eleven to thirteen years.

5

Dalmatian history

Dalmatians have worked for people for hundreds of years! In the 1600s, dalmatians were **coach dogs** in England. Coach dogs were dogs that ran beside **coaches**, or carriages, like the one shown below. Horses pulled the coaches, and people rode in them. Dalmatians ran beside the coaches to protect the people inside from robbers. In the late 1700s, people brought dalmatians to the United States to be coach dogs.

Dalmatians to the rescue!

Hundreds of years ago, firefighters rode to fires in coaches. Dalmatians ran ahead of the coaches to clear paths through crowds of people. They also went inside burning buildings to help firefighters find trapped people. Today, many fire departments have dalmatians as **mascots**. A mascot is something that brings good luck.

The right pet for you?

Dalmatians are friendly dogs that can make good family pets. Dalmatians are not the right dogs for every family, however. They are a very **energetic** dog breed, so they need a lot of exercise every day. Dalmatians also grow quickly, so they are big, even while they are still young. If small children live in your home, a young dalmatian will easily knock them over.

Are you ready?

Before adding a dalmatian to your family, gather everyone together and answer the questions below.

- Dalmatians **shed**, or lose, a lot of fur. You will have to vacuum up the fur in your home regularly. To help your pet shed less fur, you will have to brush its coat every day.

- Dalmatians love attention. Will you make sure your pet gets all the attention it needs?

- Who will feed your dog every day?

- Dalmatians need a lot of exercise every day. Is your family prepared to care for an energetic dalmatian?

- **Training** a dalmatian can take a lot of time. Are you willing to work hard training your pet?

Dalmatians love toys! Will you play with your pet every day?

A place to play

Do you live in a big house with a fenced-in yard? If so, your home is perfect for a dalmatian! Dalmatians should not live in small homes, such as apartments. They run around their homes a lot. In small places, dalmatians can hurt themselves and damage the belongings of their owners.

Your dalmatian will enjoy exploring your yard.

Running and jumping

A home that has a fenced-in yard will allow a dalmatian to run around without being tied up. Dalmatians are great jumpers, however! The fence must be at least six to eight feet (2-2.5 m) high, or your pet may jump over it.

Your dalmatian should not be left outdoors all the time. If it is left in the yard, the dog will bark all day. It may also dig holes. Bring your pet inside so that it can be a part of your family.

Dalmatians need exercise!

Dalmatians can run for hours without becoming tired! They need more exercise than most other dogs need. Even if your dalmatian spends time playing in your yard, you must take it for a long walk every day. Are you willing to spend an hour every day walking your dalmatian, even in cold or rainy weather?

Part of the family

Exercising your dalmatian does not have to be unpleasant! Dalmatians are great dogs for families that love outdoor activities. Allow your dalmatian to take part in your family's activities. Your dalmatian will be happy to join your family on walks, bike rides, hiking trips, and any other outdoor fun.

Your dalmatian can join you in many outdoor activities.

Spotted puppies

Dalmatian **puppies** are cute! A puppy is a baby dog. When they are born, dalmatian puppies have white fur. They start to get spots when they are about two weeks old. Dalmatian puppies are fun, curious, and playful. They are difficult to take care of, however. Puppies need people around them all the time. They need to be fed many times a day.

Many feedings

If you have a puppy, feed it dry food made for puppies. Add some hot water to your puppy's food to make it softer. Let the food cool down before giving it to your puppy! Feed your puppy four times a day until it is four months old. At four months old, your puppy should eat dry food three times a day. When your puppy is six months old, feed it dry food twice a day.

Housebreaking your dog

You will have to **housebreak** your dalmatian puppy. Dogs that are housebroken know to go to the bathroom outdoors. To housebreak your puppy, put it on its leash and take it outdoors about ten minutes after it eats or drinks. Take your puppy to the same place each time. Praise your puppy when it is finished. If you are **consistent** in the training, your puppy will learn to get your attention when it needs to go outdoors.

Picking your pet

You can get your dalmatian from many places. Before you buy a dog, ask your friends and **veterinarian**, or "vet," if they know of any dalmatians that are being given away. Then check **animal shelters** in your area to see if they have any dalmatians. You can also get a dalmatian from a **breeder** or a pet store. Make sure you get your pet from people who take good care of animals!

Proof in the papers

Do you want a **purebred** dalmatian? A purebred dog has parents and grandparents of the same breed. If you want proof that your dalmatian is purebred, get your pet from a breeder. A breeder should give you papers that prove your dalmatian's parents and grandparents were also dalmatians.

Choosing a healthy dalmatian

Make sure you choose a dalmatian that is healthy and seems to like you. The dog you choose should have:

- no sores on its skin
- a clean coat, snout, and bottom
- a smooth, shiny coat with no bald patches
- clean teeth
- clear, shiny eyes
- clean ears with no wax inside
- a lot of energy
- a friendly, playful personality

Spend time with a dalmatian before choosing it as your pet. Make sure it is healthy and friendly.

Preparing for your pet

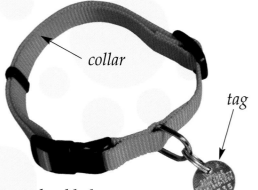

collar

tag

Your pet should always wear a **collar** with a **tag**. The tag has your telephone number on it. Your vet can also use a needle to place a small **microchip** with your address in it under your dog's skin. People can use the tag or microchip to return your pet to you if it gets lost.

You will need a lot of supplies to care for your dalmatian properly. Make sure you have all these supplies before you bring home your new pet.

Your dalmatian will need a bowl for water and another bowl for food.

A big dog like a dalmatian is easier to walk if it is wearing a **harness**. The harness wraps around your dalmatian's body.

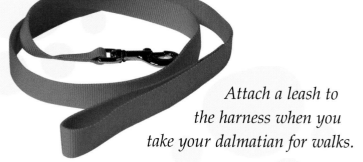

Attach a leash to the harness when you take your dalmatian for walks.

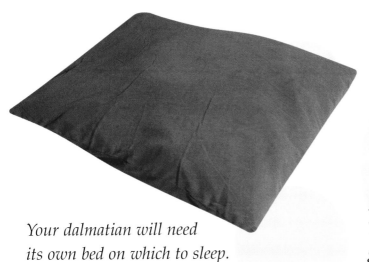

Your dalmatian will need
its own bed on which to sleep.

Dalmatians have thick, rough coats.
You will need a soft **bristle brush** to
groom, or clean, your dalmatian's coat.

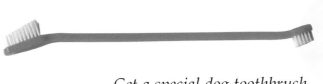

Get a special dog toothbrush
and toothpaste to keep your
dalmatian's teeth healthy.

Buy some treats for your
pet. Use the treats as rewards
when you train your dog.

Special **nail clippers** will allow
you to trim your pet's nails.

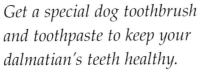

Your dalmatian should
always have toys to play
with and to chew.

Your dalmatian will use a **crate** as a quiet
den, or a place in which to relax and feel safe.

Healthy meals

Your dalmatian may need a special diet in order to stay healthy. Some dalmatians develop hard stones in their **bladders** if they eat certain types of dog food. The bladder is an important body part. Having stones in their bladders is very dangerous for dalmatians. Your dalmatian should eat foods made from **poultry** or lamb, rather than **red meats**, such as beef. Never feed your dalmatian **organ meats** or **game**.

Two feedings

If your dalmatian is an adult, feed it twice each day. Ask your vet which kind of food is healthiest for your pet. Your vet can also tell you how much food to give your dalmatian at each feeding.

Make sure your dalmatian always has fresh water to drink. Wash its water and food bowls every day.

Unhealthy foods

Never feed your dalmatian anything but its pet food. Many foods that humans eat can make dalmatians very sick. Some of these foods are listed below.

- Do not feed your dalmatian red meats.
- Do not feed your pet **dairy foods**.
- Never give your dog bones to chew.
- Never feed your dalmatian **raw** meat or raw eggs.
- Do not feed your dog even small amounts of chocolate.

Training tips

Spend time every day training your dalmatian. Dalmatians learn things quickly, but they like to be in control! Even after your pet has learned a **command**, or instruction, it may test you by not always obeying the command. Be consistent in the training, and your pet will learn to obey you every time.

Sit!

You should teach your pet basic commands, such as "sit." Use treats to help your pet learn. Show your dalmatian a treat. Hold the treat over your dog's head and say "sit." Your dalmatian should sit down to look up at the treat. When your dalmatian sits, give it the treat and a lot of praise.

Be patient while your pet learns. Praise your pet every time it obeys you. Never hit your dog or yell at it!

Getting help

Take your dalmatian to **obedience school**, or a school in which dogs are trained. The trainers at the school can help you train even the most challenging dalmatian! At the school, your dalmatian will have to spend time around other dogs. Dalmatians rarely like other dogs. You have to train your pet to accept them.

Ask a trainer at the obedience school to help you introduce your dalmatian to other dogs.

Good grooming

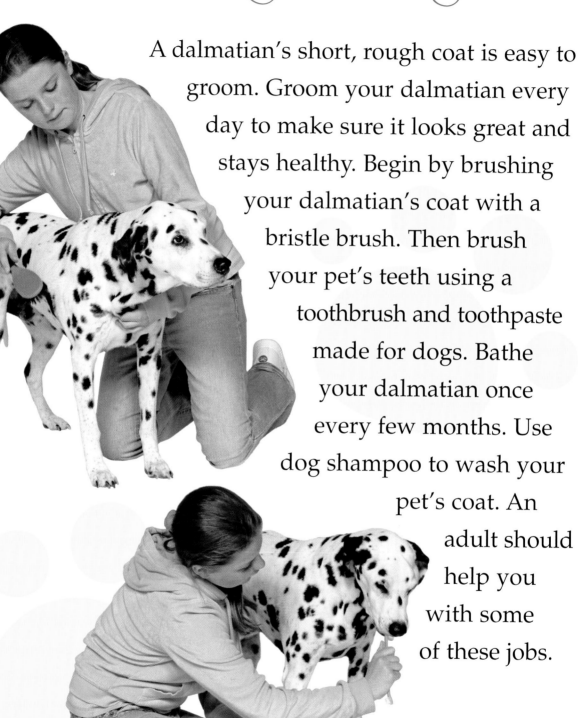

A dalmatian's short, rough coat is easy to groom. Groom your dalmatian every day to make sure it looks great and stays healthy. Begin by brushing your dalmatian's coat with a bristle brush. Then brush your pet's teeth using a toothbrush and toothpaste made for dogs. Bathe your dalmatian once every few months. Use dog shampoo to wash your pet's coat. An adult should help you with some of these jobs.

Ears and eyes

Every day, wipe the undersides of your pet's ears gently with a damp cloth. Then look inside the ears. If you see redness, sores, or a lot of wax in the ears, take your dog to the vet. Next, look into your dalmatian's eyes. Make sure the eyes are not red and that there is no dirt in them.

Nifty nails

Ask an adult to trim your pet's nails using nail clippers made for dogs. Only a small section at the end of each nail should be trimmed. If too much of the nail is cut, it will bleed. Use **styptic powder** to stop the bleeding. If your dog's nails continue to bleed, take your pet to the vet right away.

Play is important!

Dalmatians like to chase things and chew on them. Balls and other toys made of tough rubber are great for dalmatians! Give your pet about five toys at a time. Keep other toys tucked away. Once a month, switch the toys to keep your dog interested in them. If your pet has a favorite toy, make sure you do not take that one away!

Do not give your dalmatian hard plastic toys that can break into pieces when it chews them. Your pet may choke on the pieces. Any soft toys you give your pet should be filled with soft material, not beads. Remove plastic parts from soft toys before giving them to your dog.

Go get it!

Dalmatians love to play **fetch**. To play fetch, throw a Frisbee or a ball in a fenced-in area. Your dalmatian will run to get it. Train your dalmatian to give the toy back to you. Your dalmatian will want you to chase it to get the toy. This is a fun game for the dalmatian, but it will not help you train your dog. By chasing the dalmatian, you make the toy seem special, so your pet will want to keep it. Instead of chasing your dalmatian, point your finger at the ground and say "drop." If your dalmatian drops the toy, give it a lot of praise. At first, you may have to use treats to get your pet to drop its toy.

Staying safe

Your dalmatian will love spending time with you, but there are times when you should not bother your dog. For example, your dalmatian may become **aggressive**, or angry, if you bother it while it eats. The dog may bite you to protect its food. Allow your pet to finish its meal. Your dalmatian will be happy to play with you when it is finished eating.

Do not bother your pet while it is resting in its crate or on its bed. After its rest, your dog will be ready to play.

Warning!

Your dalmatian may warn you when it is angry. It may stare at you and growl. If your pet behaves this way, do not run away or yell at your dog. This behavior may make your pet more angry. Instead, stand very still and hold your arms at your sides. Do not look your pet in the eyes. Say "good dog" in a soothing voice to try to calm down the dog. When the dog calms down, tell an adult how the dog behaved.

Guilty smiles

Did you know that dalmatians can smile? Your dalmatian may look aggressive when it smiles, but it is not angry. Dalmatians smile when they are nervous or when they feel guilty. They often smile when they have done something naughty!

To the vet!

Take your new pet to the vet for a checkup to make sure it is healthy. You dalmatian may need **vaccinations**. The vet will give the dog vaccinations with needles. Take your dalmatian to the vet for a checkup every year. Dalmatians often develop certain health problems, such as stones in their bladders. Many dalmatians become **deaf** soon after they are born. A deaf dog cannot hear. If your pet is having trouble hearing you, take it to the vet right away.

No unwanted puppies!

There are many dogs in animal shelters that do not have homes. Do not add to this problem! Have your dalmatian **neutered**. A neutered dog cannot make puppies. If you do let your dalmatian have puppies, you must find good homes for all the puppies.

Be aware

If your dalmatian seems sick, take it to the vet right away. Your pet may be sick if:

- it is vomiting, fainting, or limping.

- it is losing large clumps of fur.

- it has lumps on its body, or if its ears and eyes are not clean.

- it is drinking more water than usual or if it is not eating any food.

- it is sleeping a lot and if it is not playful.

Lasting friendship

Dalmatians are smart, energetic dogs that love people. They make great pets! With proper care, your dalmatian will be a part of your family for many years.

Words to know

Note: Boldfaced words that are defined in the book may not appear on this page.

animal shelter A place that cares for animals that do not have owners

breeder A person who brings dogs together so the dogs can make puppies

consistent Describing behavior that does not change over time

dairy food Food made with milk and milk products

energetic Describes a person or an animal that has a lot of energy

game Meat from wild animals, such as deer or rabbit, which people hunt for food

microchip A small device that can be placed under an animal's skin and that holds information

organ meat Meat from an animal's organ, such as the liver

poultry Meat from birds, such as chickens, turkeys, or ducks, that people raise for food

raw Describes uncooked food

styptic powder A powder used to stop bleeding

train To teach your dog how to behave properly

vaccination A way of protecting a body against certain diseases

veterinarian A doctor who treats animals

Index

Printed in the U.S.A.